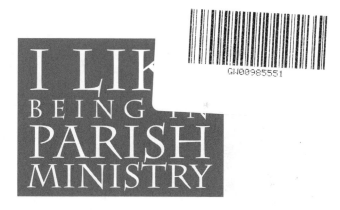

Lector

Alice Camille

TWENTY-THIRD PUBLICATIONS
A Division of Bayard   MYSTIC, CT 06355

Twenty-Third Publications
A Division of Bayard
185 Willow Street
P.O. Box 180
Mystic, CT 06355
(860) 536-2611
(800) 321-0411
www.twentythirdpublications.com

ISBN:1-58595-150-1
Printed in the U.S.A.

Contents

Introduction

So you're thinking about being a lector! Maybe someone approached you at church about the idea. Or you read an item in the parish bulletin about the need for lectors, and you felt a twinge of interest. It could be that you listened, spellbound, as a particularly able lector made an old reading sound fresh and open to you for the first time. You were stirred by the experience, and wished you could be part of that ministry. Or you may have heard lectors race through the readings like they had a plane to catch. You thought to yourself, "I could do better than that!"

On the one hand, something has piqued your curiosity about the business of lectoring. But there's that nagging fear of public performance that psychologists say is an almost universal experience. Reading in public puts us all back in the second grade, when Miss Kiley called on us to stand in the front of the room and read for the class. We were half proud, half petrified at the idea of just being visible to so many people. Why should you put yourself through that anxiety again, especially if you don't have to?

Demystifying the role may help to lessen the fear. Lectoring is not an honor bestowed on the worthy, but a service offered to the community. Like any other role we may play in the Sunday assembly—from the soprano in the choir to the participant in the last pew—the lector is giving his or her gift for the sake of the whole gathering. Although it may feel like it's "all about you"

when you're up there at the microphone, at least at first, it may help reduce your anxiety to realize that what you are doing is performing a service role as vital and natural as the one played by the person who vacuumed the church carpets on Saturday. This particular service assists the community at prayer by helping them to hear the word of God a little more clearly. But you don't have to be special to do it.

This book offers both spiritual and practical considerations about the service of the lector. It is arranged in short chapters followed by some questions for personal reflection or group discussion. Each chapter also includes a prayer suggestion and Scripture to help you consider how you are a bearer of God's word to others.

Thanks to the Reilly family—Mary, Amanda, Megan, and Ida—and Elaine Yastishock and Anya Artigiani for their reflections on why they like to lector. We are grateful for your voices.

THE
POWER
OF
WORDS

I n this country, most of us have been reading since we were
six. The miracle of literacy is commonplace. The magic of
symbols on a page, revealing the thoughts of a whole civi-
lization, escapes us. Newspapers clutter our tables, and junk mail
spills over every surface. Books are stacked unceremoniously
around the house. "Words, words, words," Hamlet once sighed.
They're on cereal boxes, billboards, tee shirts, and bumper stick-
ers. Words are so prevalent, we are nearly indifferent to them.

We forget that, for most of human history, the ability to read
was limited to the privileged few. Those who possessed the skill
of reading and writing had access to the collective knowledge of
the ages. The rest of the community relied on these scribes and
scholars to tell them what the law said, what the ancient wisdom
was, and what the stories of their ancestors described. Early lec-

tors, we could say, were powerful and valuable people within the community.

In our modern world, the public reader does not necessarily possess a unique gift within the community. Almost any member of the assembly can do what he or she does. In fact, we could dispense with lectors altogether, pass out the pertinent passages to the assembly at large, and ask all who have gathered to read it for themselves. Why not do it this way? Would it make a difference, for example, if we read the readings at home before we came to Mass, or sat silently and read them to ourselves at the beginning of the liturgy?

The difference between the written word and the spoken one becomes apparent as soon as we float the idea of dismissing the lectors. Both written and spoken words communicate, but each vehicle makes use of words differently. In writing, the words stand alone. They speak for themselves. In a sense, written words are invincible because they remain on the page whether you like them or not. That's why writing is such a powerful art, and why writers suffer oppression in lands where ideas must be controlled. "The pen is mightier than the sword," as the saying goes. Written words are hard to stop. You may imprison or execute the writer, but the words go on and on.

The spoken word has a face

Stronger than an army, longer-lived than Methuselah, the written word is an impenetrable force. It carries our history and shapes our future with its wisdom and warning. The written word also holds the measure of our dreams as a people and communicates them down through the generations.

But compare that with the spoken word! Speaking is a finite exercise, locked into a moment of time. It necessarily involves a person, immediate and specific. Although written words can mask the writer in anonymity, the speaker must step out from behind the words and present his or her own self. The spoken word, associated with a particular person, is much more vulnerable. It is part message, part testimony. The speaker is the medium for the message, and as Marshall McLuhan said, the medium is the message.

While a written word requires merely an idea coupled with language, a spoken word demands energy and charisma to get the idea across. It involves not simply words, but the performance of words. We could say it is a word made flesh. And in the Christian tradition, we don't take incarnate words lightly. Because Jesus became God's-word-made-flesh for us, we know that a word only fully reveals its meaning when it takes on flesh. We have learned that we can touch God better when the divine word has a human face.

In a way, we recreate the mystery of incarnation twice in every liturgy: once in the consecration, and also in the proclamation of the Scriptures. In the proclamation, however, the word of God takes on flesh through the minister of the word, our lector.

Talk about holding a treasure in earthen vessels! The lector, even while he or she struggles over the pronunciation of ancient Hebrew lands and peoples, is presenting the human face of God's revealing word. As one lector puts it, "I try to empty myself so I can be open to whatever God wants to communicate through me." And if the lector can do it, the whole assembly sees that the human face of God is one we are each invited to present to the world.

Giving voice to the word

The word of God has never come into the world without a face. In the record of Scripture, God always chose a person to go with the message. The original messengers of God's word were called *nabi*, a Hebrew word meaning "the mouthpiece of God." We are more familiar with them as the prophets.

The word prophet comes from the Greek term *pro-phetes*, "one who speaks on behalf of the gods." We commonly use the word prophet to mean someone who can predict the future. But biblical prophets were less involved with the future and more interested in interpreting the past and speaking directly to the present. They were not concerned with fortunetelling, but with pointing out where things were headed if the people remained on their present course.

The prophets didn't act on their own initiative. They didn't compose sermons to read in the assembly, or present their own agenda. Rather, they saw their business principally as a delivery service. First, they listened for God's word themselves. Then, they got up the courage to deliver the message.

Of course, even the biblical prophets had their performance issues. Moses protested to God that he had a speech impediment which made him a poor messenger. Isaiah claimed he was an unworthy man and should not be considered for the job. Jeremiah said he was too young, perhaps not yet twenty according to Scripture scholars. Amos made it very clear when he delivered the divine word that he was only a shepherd, and prophecy was not his day job.

We even have the story of Jonah, a fictional prophet who heard the call of God to prophesy to the people of the north. So he promptly got into a boat and headed south, hoping to escape the invitation. None of these prophets, real or fictional, were able to elude their service. It seems God does not accept our weaknesses or imagined inadequacies as an excuse to let us off the hook.

As a lector I know says it: "I get shy. I get scared. Sometimes I hear my voice cracking. Then I have to remind myself: it's okay, it's not about me. It's about the word. I know I am prepared because I have read the readings many, many times. Sometimes I have cried with them. And I know that the people hear what God needs for them to hear. Like the man who came up to me a few weeks ago and said, 'I really enjoy when you read, because when you do, I don't feel like sleeping.'" For a lector, that's success!

FOR YOUR REFLECTION

- Name something you have read that moved or persuaded you at a deep level. Can you name stories from the Bible that have had a similar effect on you?

- The spoken word is partly about content, and partly a personal testimony. What makes a person's testimony credible to you? What factors detract from a speaker's credibility?

- Jesus is God's word made flesh. What is the relationship between your word—that is, what you say—and how you live?
- Think of a time you had to speak publicly about something that was important to you. How does the process of saying something out loud and in public change the speaker?
- Who are our modern prophets? How does our society choose among the many voices clamoring for our attention?

WAYS TO RESPOND

- Look around your home and make note of some of the words that you have chosen to live with. They may be on tee shirts, posters, in frames, or taped to the refrigerator. What impact do these words have on you and others, and what do they reveal about your values?
- Consider adding a favorite Scripture passage to the words you regularly live with. It may be something that strikes you personally at Mass this week, or a quote you've long loved. Pin it to your bulletin board at work or fix it to a mirror at home.

FOR YOUR PRAYER

O God, Lover of us all, you have shown your love to us in your word made flesh, Jesus Christ. He is your heart, your soul, your mind and your strength. Bless those who love you and whom you have called to proclaim your word and preside at your table. May we joyfully celebrate your presence in our lives this Sunday, both in word and in sacrament. Amen.

SHAPED BY TRADITION

I t must be admitted that there are some differences between the prophet of old and today's lector. The biblical prophet had to listen intently for God's word in the desert and on city streets. He or she (and there were prophetesses, like Deborah in the Book of Judges, or Anna in the Gospel of Luke) had to be able to discern God's hand in the movement of a foreign army, or the subtleties of a blossoming branch. A prophet had to capture God's words whispered in the air in order to proclaim them.

The contemporary lector has a written text of God's word on which to rely. The book of readings used in church, called the lectionary, ensures that the entire Catholic community throughout the world is "on the same page," every day of the year. The lectionary has its roots in the practices of the Jewish community. The idea was to assign certain readings from the Scriptures to be read according to the feast or season. Jesus made use of his version of the lectionary when he read in front of the assembly in Nazareth (see Luke 4).

Before the Council of Nicea in 325 CE, the church had a formal lectionary only for special feasts of the church year. On Sundays, particular books of the Bible were read in small, continuous sections week after week until they were finished. The original Liturgy of the Word—the first part of Mass up to and including the homily—included several lessons from both the Hebrew Scripture (Old Testament) and Christian Scripture (New Testament), with psalms sung in between. By the sixth century, the Roman practice was to read only one passage from each testament, along with a psalm.

Our present habit of using two readings, a psalm, and a gospel passage on Sundays comes from the revised lectionary of 1969. We follow a three-year cycle in which we hear from Matthew (cycle A), Mark (cycle B), and Luke (cycle C) for a year at a time. Sections of John appear at special times throughout the three years. On weekdays, we follow a two-year cycle of readings, and listen to two Scripture readings plus the psalm at each Mass.

Every Catholic, and especially every lector, ought to become familiar with the pattern of the readings as we move from year to year and season to season. The more we understand the movement of the lectionary through the church year, the better we hear the message being delivered to us.

Claiming and proclaiming

The biblical prophets didn't have a lectionary to guide them in presenting God's word to the people. But they did have something else in common with the modern lector. They had to enter into relationship with the word they heard and make it their own.

What does it mean to have a personal relationship with the divine word? It begins with the idea of incarnation. The medium is the message; or, we are the message we bear. This is true for every Christian, but it starts with the sincerity of the message-bearer. Nothing erodes the morale of a community the way religious hypocrisy does. "Practice what you preach" goes into the same box as "Physician, heal thyself." In order to bring the medicine to the people, you have to show some evidence that the medicine works. That evidence is you.

Prophets wrestled with the word of God, sometimes literally like Jacob, who once pinned an angel to the ground who brought him a message from his Maker. And prophets suffered the effects of delivering the divine word. Jeremiah was thrown into a muddy cistern and left to starve because what he said made people uncomfortable. He was later rescued by order of the king, but not all prophets were so fortunate. Jesus mentions several times that the people of God regularly put the prophets of God to death, right in Jerusalem, God's holy city.

Stephen became the first martyr of the church because he offended the crowds with his honesty, not to mention his accuracy. Paul lists a litany of complaints he suffered for the sake of the word, including being beaten, driven out of town, shipwrecked, arrested, and stoned and left for dead. Today's lectors have it easier in that they are proclaiming God's word only to the willing assembly. Few modern lectors have been arrested or beaten for their proclamation. And that includes the worst lectors you've ever heard!

But still, the task remains: to make the word a part of your life in a deep and central way. A woman who lectors at an urban church says, "The honor of proclaiming the Scripture to the assembly—and especially to myself—recommits me to my own faith. I will never forget the lector training I received from a professor of rhetoric at a nearby university. He had us stand outside in pairs, fifty feet from one another as we proclaimed. The person listening would yell out the following statements whenever he or she felt they were true: "I don't hear you!" "I don't understand you!" "I don't believe you!" That last measure, being believable and speaking with conviction, may be the greatest test of all.

FOR YOUR REFLECTION

- When in your life have you "sensed" God's will for you through sign more clearly than in words? How does the church's use of Scripture and sacrament work together to reveal God's message?
- What are your favorite feasts and seasons in the church year? How does the movement of the church year help you to pray?
- Can you name the parts of the Liturgy of the Word? (You may want to check a missalette or Catholic missal for verification.) How do these elements work together to help the assembly attend to the Scriptures?
- Does the Bible wield an authority in your life? What claim does Scripture have on the values you live by, and the decisions you make?
- Would you be willing to be a lector if you were held personally responsible for the words you proclaimed to the assembly?

WAYS TO RESPOND

- Become more familiar with the lectionary and the cycles of the church year. You may want to spend some time with the lectionary in your parish, or acquire a lectionary-based study guide that helps you follow the movement of the church year. Read the gospel for this year in its entirety, a few paragraphs a day. Notice the themes and patterns that emerge when you hear the story continuously.
- Listen to the readings at Mass next Sunday as if they were written deliberately and specifically for you.

Contemplate how this word from God strengthens, supports, or challenges you.

FOR YOUR PRAYER

O Lord, you speak your word of life in me to protect me from harm and guide me to fulfillment. This day I have lived in your word and I rejoice and give you thanks. This day I have also abandoned your word and I am sorry. Keep me alive in your love. Show me the path made bright by your word, for all my hope is in you. Amen.

AT
YOUR
SERVICE

The word of God is given to us for our use. But more importantly, we who attend to it are at the service of the word. One of the many gifts of being a lector is how directly and immediately we experience that truth. Lectoring is about serving the assembly, but also about being of service to God's word. Like a good chauffeur, the lector can't just drive up to the church, drop off the word of God and head off into the sunset. A taxi driver disappears the moment the service is paid for, but a chauffeur stays close. The chauffeur remains in service even when not playing an active role. Staying close to the word, even when not actively serving the community as a lector, is part of the vocation of a servant of the word.

Naturally, service to the word is the responsibility of every Christian and not simply the one who proclaims it. A subtle change in usage during the liturgy was made in the last generation to underscore this idea. At one time, the lector concluded the reading by lifting the book and saying, "This is the word of the Lord." Similarly, the minister of the Eucharist offered the host with the words, "This is the body of Christ." Both of these terms focused our attention on the elements of word and sacrament, the book and the host, as if God's holy presence was contained solely within them.

In the revised liturgy, the lector now finishes the reading by saying, "The word of the Lord!" just as the eucharistic minister says, "The body of Christ!" A small change in words, perhaps, but a wider shift in intent. The word of the Lord, once proclaimed, is no longer bound to the pages of a book but roams unfettered in our midst. Having attended to the word, we now dwell in it as it lives in us. It is the same way that we become incorporated into Christ's body even as we incorporate it into our bodies.

The task of every Christian is to become the presence of God for others, and the vocation of the lector is to present the word to the assembly as its first faithful servant. It doesn't mean the lector is or must be the most pious person in church. But faithful service to the word has a way of growing on you. The call to lectoring is a conscious call to walk a little closer to that word.

Companioning the Word

How do lectors prepare for their service to the word and to the assembly? The most natural way is to keep company with the Scriptures. Don't be a stranger. Get comfortable with the Bible, its language, its history, and its story. There are many ways of doing this, depending on your personality and learning style.

If you are a people-person, you may want to join a Bible study, get involved with a lectionary-based reading circle with the other lectors or liturgical ministers at your church, or become a catechist for the RCIA process. Spending regular time with the Scriptures from week to week will help you get a feel for the way the story is told and who the principal characters are. Remember, if it sounds like Greek to you when you read it over yourself, it's going to be Greek to the assembly when you read it on Sunday. Understanding what's happening and who-did-what-to-whom is important in storytelling and proclamation.

If you are a bookish type, there are many great resources available to assist you (some of which are listed at the end of this book.) Start by getting a copy of the Bible for your own personal use. Don't rely on the twenty-pound Douay-Rheims coffee table Bible with gold edges and full-color plates for your preparation. Get an inexpensive paperback, preferably one marked "study edition," with good footnotes. Now, this may strike the especially pious folks with squeamishness, but make up your mind that it's okay to write in this one. As you read along, underline ideas that seem key to you, or especially beautiful or personally meaningful. Make question marks next to things that are troubling and hard to understand so that you can look them up later in another resource for more information.

A Bible commentary is also very helpful. Many public libraries will have a hardbound set of these, each volume dedicated to a different book of the Bible. You can also subscribe to an ongoing lectionary-based service for your own use fairly cheaply. Chances are your pastor will even pay for it!

Finally, the standard research tools for anyone seriously interested in getting a handle on the Scriptures are a lexicon or concordance, and a small manual of biblical pronunciations. A lexicon helps you to find any word that appears in the Bible. Its alphabetical listing is like a dictionary, and so you can find just about any phrase so long as you can remember a word or two of it. You can also find passages that are related to the same concept, which can be helpful when you really want to understand what a covenant is, or to find all the stories in which Peter appears in the gospels. A concordance is similar to a lexicon, but only contains key names and concepts, not every single word. A manual of pronunciation helps you to avoid making the worst lector bloopers, like saying "brassiere" when you mean "brazier."

Making the Commitment

At my parish, they hand out twenty-seven pages of notes to every new lector, and much of it is about scheduling: where to find the lector mailbox, rosters, keeping your address current on the lector list, what to do in case of substitutions, no-shows, sign-in sheets, and how to apply for "lector leave!" This may seem formidable to the new lector, and it may not be this elaborate in every parish. But it does illustrate the commitment involved in becoming a parish lector.

Some parishes "install" lectors with a formal ceremony each year, calling them forward at Mass and distributing a special blessing before the whole community. In some dioceses, the commitment is made at the cathedral, elevating the commissioning to a service on behalf of the bishop. At one time in the church's history, the lector was actually a formal stage in a seminarian's preparation for holy orders. All of this underscores the idea that lectoring is a serious commitment to make, and should not be taken half-heartedly.

And yet, being a lector really requires very simple things: a willingness to serve, a short period of preparation in advance of each reading, and the good grace to show up on time at the Mass at which you are scheduled to read. Some parishes offer lector-training workshops for an evening or two, to assist you with practical matters like knowing how to turn on the microphone and where the lectionary is kept when not in use. Each lector should have the opportunity to test the mike and practice with a coach, who can tell if someone's voice is projecting clearly or if reading faster or slower is indicated.

Your parish may have a dress code for liturgical ministers in general—common sense prevails here. Save your threadbare "lucky" jeans and the sweatshirt that didn't make it into last week's laundry for a less public occasion. A suit or a dress may not be necessary, but a clean and neat appearance registers respect for your service to the word and to the assembly.

Finally, the most fundamental aspect of your commitment is to show up when you are scheduled. Conflicts and emergencies will arise from time to time preventing you from your service. So be sure to have the names and phone numbers of who to call when this occurs. Most parishes provide each lector with a current list of substitutes.

When parishes consider who should be invited to lector, young people should not be overlooked. Children lectors—and every parochial school produces them—are some of the best, because they approach the ministry very seriously. "Lectoring is special!" a first-grader tells me, "I feel good when I talk loud and clear. I think it is important." A girl in the fifth grade has advice about preparation: "I practice at home for a few weeks before. I practice so that when I go to speak in the microphone, my voice doesn't fade off. I also want to be sure that I understand what I'm reading."

A junior high student recognizes the active role of the assembly in what she is doing: "Hopefully, everyone is listening." She is not unfamiliar with technical trouble. "I remember last year, the microphone failed us and I had to read (scream!) the opening without it." This experience hasn't deterred her from persevering. And when the kids read, the adults sit up and listen. And if the parents lector, the children watch and learn something about what it means to be vitally present to the liturgy. "I am always honored to participate in the Mass in any capacity," a mother explains. "As a speech therapist, it is already my vocation to help others to improve their communication skills, so lectoring would naturally be attractive to me." It is no wonder that her children enjoy lectoring too.

FOR YOUR REFLECTION

- How can you be at the service of God's word in your family, at work, in the community? How does your parish demonstrate that the entire assembly is at the service of God's word, both in the liturgy and outside of it?

- How familiar or unfamiliar are you with the stories of the Bible? How have you acquired your main experience of the Bible: parochial school education, parish religious education classes, hearing the readings at Mass, personal Scripture reading, group study, or some other source?

- How reliable are you at keeping your commitments? When you make a commitment, do you follow through with your responsibilities?

- How willing are you to hear constructive criticism about what you do? From whom are you willing to receive such advice?

- How does the physical appearance of a lector, in dress, posture, and comportment, affect you as you listen? How do you think a lector should present himself or herself?

WAYS TO RESPOND

- Practice reading aloud some of the most energy-laden passages from the Bible, like John the Baptist's sermon at the Jordan (Matthew 3:7–12), or Jesus' denunciation of the religious leaders (Luke 11:39–52). Learn to harness the natural force of these passages for your proclamation.

- Make a commitment to learn more about the Bible. Introductory sessions to the Bible are often taught in parishes. Check to see what yours or a neighboring parish has to offer. Or visit the parish library, your diocesan media center, or a Catholic bookstore to find books and videos that may help you in your personal reading of Scripture. (See also Resources for Further Reading at the end of this book.)

O God, from the beginning you have always kept your promises. Let your word echo through my life, in my thoughts, words, and deeds. Keep me ever mindful of the commitments I have made. May I be a good witness of the word you have spoken.

PERFORMANCE HINTS

B eing a lector is not the same as being an actor. But there are performance aspects to any public role, and the liturgical assembly is no exception. Some factors affecting our performance are out of our control. We can control the way we dress, but not the way we look. We can learn to work with the microphone for better volume, but we can't change the way our voice sounds. We can learn how to carry the Book of the Gospels in procession, but we may never be as graceful as Baryshnikov when we do it.

The fact that we are flawed people who can (and do) make mistakes is part of the reality of life. So if you are going to be a lector, get used to the idea that errors will be part of the experience.

Bad things happen to good lectors. Temperamental mikes start squealing. Sirens wailing outside the church eclipse your voice.

The person who read before you turned to the wrong page. And sometimes you just lose your place. Make sure you know whose responsibility it is to adjust the mike when there's a problem—yours? The sacristan's? Make sure you note the page your reading begins on before the service starts, so finding it won't be a nightmare for you or the assembly, even if the book gets dropped. (And it does get dropped.)

And if you are particularly worried about tripping on the stairs on the way into the sanctuary, wear sensible shoes that decrease that possibility. But falling down, even if it happens, is not the end of the world. I've seen priests faint at the altar and deacons do a nosedive during the procession, book, ribbons, and all. Unless someone is hurt, generally a few moments is all it takes to get up and continue the liturgy. The assembly is a very forgiving place. If you can't get a little sympathy and support here, it could be time to find another parish!

Unless you have a serious vocal impairment or a voice that sounds like a Warner Brothers cartoon character, you can probably learn to lector. Be open to critiques on your performance. It's good for your humility to recognize that you can always do better. Adjust your volume, pace, posture, and inflection at the advice of someone you trust. Reduce fidgeting to a minimum. Scratch less. Breathe more deeply. Make eye contact by looking at people, and not just looking up.

The best school for lectoring, of course, is to learn from good lectors themselves. Listen to other lectors, watch what they do, and ask them for advice or to critique your performance. In this day of accessible video, if you can have yourself taped and actually see what you are doing...well, a picture is worth a thousand words.

Taking a Risk

We live in reasonably comfortable times. And yet curiously, we live in a society deeply imbedded with the inner demons of poor self-esteem. Most of us don't like to take risks, or to expose ourselves to the possibility of embarrassment. I think the most frequently reported reason that people decline the invitation to become a lector is not an unwillingness to serve, but the fear of doing something wrong.

The key to public delivery is in self-forgetfulness. Jesus once said that we had to lose our lives to save them, and that dynamic of lose-to-gain is predominant in our lives as Christians. When we lose self-consciousness, we gain self-possession. In lectoring, we lose ourselves in the word we come to proclaim, and find ourselves claimed by the power of the Spirit. There is no greater spiritual development program than to give yourself over to the Scriptures. The greatest risk we face in doing this is that we may become fully awake for the first time in our lives.

Because, when you think about it, doing something wrong during the liturgy does not make someone a bad lector. In fact, losing one's place, stammering a little, or mispronouncing something is probably the quickest way to get a little human sympathy from the assembly. I mentioned the deacon who took a bad tumble during the opening procession. I did not mention this occurred at a major conference where five bishops were co-presiding, not to mention busloads of priests, all in front of a stadium full of people and video cameras. The man may have been nervous in this context to begin with, but imagine how he felt after he sprawled face-first in the middle of it all!

But he won our hearts at once with his valiant courage as he got up, retrieved the book, and continued forward. Of course he lost the ribbon marking the page, so when it came time to read, he was in a fine mess. But the crowds were silently rooting for him every inch of the way. He had become the home team, our hero. He was humbled, embarrassed, but willing to go the distance to bring God's word to us. And when he was finally ready to make his proclamation, we hung attentively on every word.

Lectors who take risks are the ones we remember as the really good ones. At the local Newman Center, a small young woman always grabs my attention and sustains it when she reads. She has a naturally soft soprano voice, the kind that many people would say is not an asset to public speaking. But she becomes so fully identified with each proclamation that she embodies it with her passion. Recently she gave a rendition of a passage from Revelation that should have earned her a standing ovation. "I am the Alpha and the Omega, the One who is and who was and who is to come, the Almighty!" she boomed out over the assembly, this tiny person who wasn't very mighty at all. And for that moment, she made us hear the voice of God through her. This is a hard passage to declare with conviction. Many readers might wimp out and try to tone its imperial declaration down. But any other way of reading the line sounds silly. That young woman has the fire in her blood, and she uses it fearlessly in service of the word.

Speaking with Conviction

It's clear that human weakness or error doesn't make for a bad lector. The really bad stuff we hear is from the folks who don't seem to care at all about what they have come to do. Of course this can't be true, I tell myself. Maybe they mutter their way through the reading because they haven't had adequate time to prepare, or they're filling in at the last moment for someone who is absent. Maybe the passage seemed so difficult and confusing to them that they chose to drive cautiously in a neutral tone.

(I extend this same amnesty to the occasionally passionless presider, unfriendly greeter, bored eucharistic minister, and humorless music director. Sometimes all any of us needs is a vacation!) But beyond isolated lapses like these, the only real mistake a reader can make is to convey the living word of God, the voice out of the whirlwind as the Book of Job describes it, as though it were dull and noncommittal.

Passion is the mainstay of prophetic speech. Think of John the Baptist, who scarcely spoke without exclamation: "You brood of vipers!" "Repent, for the kingdom of God is at hand!" "Behold, the Lamb of God!" We should be able to name evil, summon hearts to conversion, and reveal Christ to the assembly with as much vigor.

Lector passion is especially important because assembly apathy is so rampant. I heard a preacher once call apathy our response to the "unmitigated horror of the twentieth century." He said indifference is the way we combat the fear within us. In our global awareness of human suffering, we lose our capacity to feel indignant or to care deeply about people, issues, or the quality of our common life. This "compassion fatigue" creeps into our parishes to the point where people often sit with numbed expressions, hardly conscious of whether the word given to us this week is hope from Isaiah or a warning from Amos.

In the second half of the Mass, we break and share the bread which is Christ. In the first half, our task is to break open and share God's word. In order to do that, it is necessary to break open our hearts to receive it, and that's no easy task. Outside of the Eucharist, we have found so many ways to self-medicate against feeling. Drugs and alcohol, consumerism, immersion in work or entertainment are some of the ways we escape from the world of genuine caring. Shopping and television are perhaps the two most abused substances in our culture, which enable us to numb out and disconnect from our personal lives or world reality. All these things become mantras we repeat against the suffering within or around us.

A movement toward isolation is always a move away from the gospel. Church means community and communion on a fundamental level. But in order to reach that communion, we need the rousing, disturbing, challenging force of God's word to make us ready for it. The voice of God is like a sledgehammer taken up against the wall of apathy separating us from each other. The lector's job is to wield that power, respectful of its source and convinced of its urgency.

FOR YOUR REFLECTION

- Have you ever used a microphone? Have you walked in a procession? Do you have experience in any kind of public performance? Which of these things (or others) seems the most challenging to you in the role of the lector?

- How comfortable are you in your own body? With the sound of your own voice? With the way you look? Which of these factors may most influence your functioning as a lector?
- What would be most helpful to you in the process of lector training? Who can you ask to get the training assistance you need?
- Which lectors get your attention most effectively? What do they do to make you listen?
- What are some of the things that you feel passionate about? Do you feel this same sense of passion when you proclaim the word of God?
- The role of a lector is to bring the good news of God to the people. Do you fully believe in this good news, or do you sometimes "self-medicate"—in any of the ways listed in the section above or in others—against personal suffering or the grim realities of our world? What can you do to break through the temptation of escapism?

WAYS TO RESPOND

- Public speaking can give anyone a bad case of nerves, but the more familiar it is, the less anxiety you feel. Make sure you practice your reading aloud before you stand up with your coach during lector training. Ask for help with any unfamiliar words. Practice with the microphone until you know all its idiosyncrasies and how to cope with them. Get an honest and perceptive friend to critique your performance more than once, and always be willing to accept feedback.

- Make a candid list of the things about you that would make you a good lector. (This is an exercise in self-esteem, not in humility!) Consider how God might be calling you to put those gifts at the disposal of the assembly.

FOR YOUR PRAYER

O God, you have called me to be a lector and have given me the grace to answer your call. Bless me as I rise to read. May my steps be sure, my body graceful. Keep my hands adept, my voice clear and strong, and my demeanor confident, so that your word may be proclaimed well in this assembly. Amen.

WHAT IT MEANS TO BE A LECTOR

I hope I have been able to strike a balance here. In all of this I mean to say two things, both of which I believe are true. First of all, lectoring is a simple, practical service that almost anyone can be trained to do. Pace, volume, and how to relate to the microphone are a matter of practice. Where to put the pauses, emphasis, and voice variation are intermediate skills a lector acquires over time. Eye contact really means people contact, and not just bobbing up and down like a mechanical drinking bird. The bottom line here is, proclaim the message to the people, and relate to them as well as to the word. The practicum of lectoring is teachable to anyone willing to learn and take a chance.

But the second thing I am also saying is that lectoring is serious business. Unlike the prophets of old, the modern lector doesn't have to learn lessons like "How to Hide From an Angry

Mob." But in a real way, proclaiming God's word in the assembly does put a price on your head. You choose to speak for God. You take on the responsibility of making the amazing public claim that what you proclaim is indeed "the word of the Lord." And this word of God will claim you, if you companion this word on the road awhile.

Zacchaeus, a little man who was claimed by the word in a gospel story, gave away a fortune with gratitude. The widow who put two coins in the temple box was making the same response. God's word liberates us from fear and apathy, and makes us free for thanksgiving and compassion. An encounter with God's word is a life-altering experience. And when we are changed, those around us change, and one by one we may change the world.

If the conversion of a single heart seems like a small thing with which to change the world, consider the example of Mother Teresa of Calcutta. She was so visibly claimed by the word she companioned that a Muslim man sobbed in the streets at the news of her death: "She was a source of perpetual joy!" Because she let the word change her, the lives of countless souls were radically altered.

Mother Teresa called herself a little pencil in God's hand. But others described her as a steamroller of a woman! Who's to say that a pencil in God's hand can't have the force of a steamroller when writing on the human heart? Each of us is a small pencil, writing our little story on the world. If we surrender the course of that story to God's creativity, we cannot imagine the wonders in store.

In our role as a lector, we don't have to wonder if people are attentive to the message, if the assembly is being converted, or if the world is being saved by our efforts. All we have to do, as our first and most vital service to the word of God, is to let it claim us. God will take it from there.

FOR YOUR REFLECTION

- Lectoring is simple, and it's also challenging. In what ways do you look forward to being challenged by the ministry of lectoring?
- How can you imagine your life being changed by companioning the word of God a little more closely?
- Who has brought God's word into your life by their example? Who may be looking to you for that kind of example, in your family or in the community where you live or work?

WAYS TO RESPOND

- Make up your mind to be a pencil in God's hand. Or be a steamroller, if that's more your style! Practice becoming more conscious, in every interaction and circumstance, of how God may be writing a message on the world through you.

FOR YOUR PRAYER

My God, in every age and in every generation you call women and men to proclaim your word and announce your ancient promises to the people you love. Help me now to know your word and make it my own. May I be a channel of your grace and a witness of your love and mercy, through Christ our Lord. Amen.

FOR FURTHER PRAYER

Prayer is among the most intimate forms of communica-tion, and prayer styles cannot and should not be dictated. However you feel most comfortable praying is most cer-tainly the best way for you to pray, and that includes the time you spend collecting yourself to open the Scriptures. You may want to meditate in silence at home; contemplate the presence of Christ before the tabernacle or a cross; gather with family or friends for shared spontaneous prayer; or recite more formal prayers like the rosary. Whatever you have been doing that enables you to hear God's voice best will work fine for lector preparation too.

But if you aren't engaged in any particular method of prayer or would like to try something aimed specifically at the minister of the word, here is a suggestion. When you begin your preparation with the Sunday readings, place the lectionary, the lectionary workbook, or the Bible you're using on your desk or in your lap. Place both hands on the book, close your eyes, and imagine the power of God flowing from you through your hands into the book. Visualize God within you as a glowing source of goodness and grace. Imagine the power of the Holy Spirit radiating from your center and flowing down your arms and out from your hands. God is calling you to a personal encounter with the divine word. What does God have to say to you today? What is God's message for the whole community of the church? Open the book to the passage you are studying this week and read it aloud, slowly and attentively.

You may also want to use some of the Scripture passages that follow to help you as you prepare your readings. These are natural meditations for anyone committed to the service of the word.

Hear O Israel! The Lord is our God, the Lord alone! Therefore, you shall love the Lord, your God, with all your heart, and with all your strength. Take to heart these words which I enjoin on you today. (Deuteronomy 6:4–6)

"This command is not up in the sky, that you should say, 'Who will go up in the sky to get it for us and tell us of it, that we may carry it out?....' No, it is something very near to you, already in your mouths and in your hearts; you have only to carry it out." (Deuteronomy 30:12, 14)

Then I said, "Woe is me, I am doomed! For I am a man of unclean lips, living among a people of unclean lips; yet my eyes have seen the King, the Lord of hosts!" Then one of the seraphim flew to me, holding an ember which he had taken with tongs from the altar. He touched my mouth with it. "See," he said, "now that this has touched your lips, your wickedness is removed, your sin purged." Then I heard the voice of the Lord saying, "Whom shall I send? Who will go for us?" "Here I am," I said; "send me!" (Isaiah 6:5–8)

The Lord God has given me the tongue of a teacher, that I may know how to sustain the weary with a word. Morning by morning he wakens—wakens my ear to listen as those who are taught. The Lord God has opened my ear, and I was not rebellious, I did not turn backward. (Isaiah 50:4–5)

How beautiful upon the mountains are the feet of him who brings glad tidings, announcing peace, bearing good news, announcing salvation, and saying to Zion, "Your God is King!" (Isaiah 52:7)

The word of the Lord has brought me derision and reproach all the day. I say to myself, I will not mention him, I will speak in his name no more. But then it becomes like fire burning in my heart, imprisoned in my bones; I grow weary holding it in, I cannot endure it. (Jeremiah 20:8b–9)

I will sprinkle clean water upon you to cleanse you from all your impurities, and from all your idols I will cleanse you. I will give you a new heart and place a new spirit within you, taking from your bodies your stony hearts, and giving you natural hearts. I will put my spirit within you and make you live by my statutes, careful to observe my decrees. (Ezekiel 36:25–28)

The hand of the Lord came upon me, and he led me out in the spirit of the Lord and set me in the center of the plain, which was now filled with bones. The Lord made me walk among them in every direction so that I saw how many they were on the surface of the plain. How dry they were! The Lord asked me: Son of man, can these bones come to life? "Lord God," I answered, "you alone know that." Then the Lord said to me: Prophesy over these bones, and say to them: Dry bones, hear the word of the Lord! (Ezekiel 37:1–4)

Jesus said to the tempter, "One does not live by bread alone, but by every word that comes forth from the mouth of God." (Matthew 4:4)

Jesus came to Nazareth, where he had grown up, and went according to his custom into the synagogue on the Sabbath day. He stood up to read and was handed a scroll of the prophet Isaiah. He unrolled the scroll and found the passage where it was written: "The spirit of the Lord is upon me, because God has anointed me to bring glad tidings to the poor. God has sent me to proclaim liberty to captives and recovery of sight to the blind, to let the oppressed go free, and to proclaim a year acceptable to the Lord." (Luke 4:16–19)

Rolling up the scroll, he handed it back to the attendant and sat down, and the eyes of all in the synagogue looked intently at him. He said to them, "Today this scripture passage is fulfilled in your hearing." (Luke 4:20–21)

"Now, Lord...grant to your servants to speak your word with all boldness, while you stretch out your hand to heal, and signs and wonders are performed through the name of your holy servant Jesus." When they had prayed, the place in which they were gathered together was shaken; and they were all filled with the Holy Spirit and spoke the word of God with boldness. (Acts 4:29–31)

With great power the apostles gave their testimony to the resurrection of the Lord Jesus, and great grace was upon them all. (Acts 4:33)

Let the word of Christ dwell in you richly; teach and admonish one another in all wisdom; and with gratitude in your hearts sing psalms, hymns, and spiritual songs to God. And whatever you do, in word or deed, do everything in the name of the Lord Jesus, giving thanks to God the Father through him. (Colossians 3:16–17)

Indeed, the word of God is living and effective, sharper than any two-edged sword, penetrating even between soul and spirit, joints and marrow, and able to discern reflections and thoughts of the heart. (Hebrews 4:12)

We can say with confidence, "The Lord is my helper; I will not be afraid. What can anyone do to me?" Remember your leaders, those who spoke the word of God to you; consider the outcome of their way of life, and imitate their faith. Jesus Christ is the same yesterday and today and forever. (Hebrews 13:6–8)

WAYS TO RESPOND

- Put aside a private fifteen minutes of your day for prayer and reflection. Make yourself comfortable, close your eyes and relax. Try to put the cares of the day out of your mind.

PRAYER SERVICES

Some parishes convene their lectors during training only. Others continue to meet weekly or seasonally to do their preparation for Sunday together. Here are a few outlines for group prayer rituals that can be used with and by lectors. These examples use ordinary sacramentals which can be modified or enhanced during special seasons (e.g., an Advent wreath lighting and a carol in December; ashes, a cross, or last year's braided palms during Lent). If your group meets often, the format suggested here should give way to more personalized gatherings as the lectors begin to form a more genuine community.

1.

Gather a group of lectors in your home or at the church. Arrange comfortable chairs in a circle with a small table in the center of the circle. Cover the table with a decorative cloth of the appropriate seasonal color. Place on the table an open lectionary or Bible, and a lighted candle. You may wish to add some flowers, or a loaf of home-baked bread. Provide nametags for the group with first names written in bold marker to make conversation easier.

After the customary greetings, have the people sit and begin the prayer with the Sign of the Cross.

Leader   Let us pray. (*Pause for a minute of silent reflection.*) O God of goodness, you have called us to proclaim your word in the assembly. We are not worthy, yet you have blessed us in your calling and in our response. Open our hearts to see your love at work in our lives. Grant this through Christ our Lord. Amen.

Ask each member of the group to tell what his or her reaction was when asked to be a lector. Then ask each to tell how ministering as a lector has been a blessing.

When all have had a chance to tell their stories, retrieve the candle from the table and pass it around the circle. As each member holds the candle, have all recite the following prayer printed beforehand on 3" x 5" cards:

All   Thank you Lord for calling (*recite the person's name*) to proclaim your word. Bless her/him and make her/him holy.

When the candle returns to you, replace it on the table, have the group stand, join hands and recite together the "Our Father." End with the Sign of the Cross.

2.

Gather a group of lectors in your home or at the parish. Arrange chairs in a circle with a small table in the center of the circle. Cover the table with a white cloth. Place on the table a clear glass bowl filled with water, and a sprig of fresh-cut evergreen.

Begin the prayer with the Sign of the Cross.

Leader   Let us pray. (*Pause for a minute of silent reflection.*) O God, you love the great and the small alike. You call your lowly people to be witnesses of your goodness and your will to save, and to bring life to fulfillment. Stir in us the Spirit of your passion. May we live your word fearlessly. We ask this through Christ our Lord.

Reading: Ezekiel 36:25–28 (see p. 37 for text)

Response: choral reading of Psalm 51

Divide the group in half. Alternate sides.

Side 1   Have mercy on me, God, in your goodness; in your abundant compassion blot out my offense. Wash away all my guilt; from my sin cleanse me.

Side 2   For I know my offense; my sin is always before me. Against you alone have I sinned; I have done such evil in your sight that you are just in your sentence, blameless when you condemn.

Side 1   True, I was born guilty, a sinner, even as my mother conceived me. Still, you insist on sincerity of heart; in my inmost being teach me wisdom.

Side 2   Cleanse me with hyssop, that I may be pure; wash me, make me whiter than snow.

Side 1	Let me hear sounds of joy and gladness; let the bones you have crushed rejoice. Turn away your face from my sins; blot out all my guilt.
Side 2	A clean heart create for me, God; renew in me a steadfast spirit. Do not drive me from your presence, nor take from me your holy spirit.
Side 1	Restore my joy in your salvation; sustain in me a willing spirit. I will teach the wicked your ways, that sinners may return to you.
Side 2	Rescue me from death, God, my saving God, that my tongue may praise your healing power. Lord, open my lips; my mouth will proclaim your praise.
Side 1	For you do not desire sacrifice; a burnt offering you would not accept. My sacrifice, God, is a broken spirit; God, do not spurn a broken, humbled heart.
Side 2	Make Zion prosper in your good pleasure; rebuild the walls of Jerusalem. Then you will be pleased with proper sacrifice, burnt offerings and holocausts; then bullocks will be offered on your altar.
Side 1	Glory to the Father, and to the Son, and to the Holy Spirit.
Side 2	As it was in the beginning, is now, and will be forever. Amen.

After a full minute of silent reflection, go to the table, take the sprig of evergreen and dip it in the water. Sprinkle the group, dipping the sprig liberally so that the symbol is substantial. Then all stand, join hands and recite together the "Our Father."

3.

Gather a group of lectors in your home or at the church. Tell them ahead of time that the theme of the gathering will be the Word of the Lord. Have them bring their favorite readings. Arrange comfortable chairs in a circle with a small table in the center of the circle. Cover the table with a decorative cloth of the appropriate seasonal color. Place an open lectionary on the table, or Bible. A lighted candle, some fresh-cut flowers, or a loaf of bread complete the arrangement. Unless it is a close circle of friends and acquaintances, provide nametags for the group with first names written in bold marker.

After the customary exchanges, have the people sit and begin the prayer with the Sign of the Cross.

Leader   Let us pray. (*Pause for a minute of silent reflection.*) O God, our Creator, your Spirit gives us life. You have placed your word in us, so that we might celebrate your promise in the assembly. May we discover in our hearts the word you have spoken. We ask this through Christ our Lord. Amen.

Have the members of the group take turns sharing their favorite readings and tell why they are meaningful to them.

When all have had a chance, take the candle from the table and pass it around the circle. As each member holds the candle, all recite the following prayer printed beforehand on 3" x 5" cards:

All   God of heaven and earth, bless your servant (recite the person's name) in whom you have placed your word. May she/he be the Word of the Lord to your people.

When the candle comes back to you, return it to the table, have the group stand, join hands and recite together the "Our Father." End with the Sign of the Cross.

Resources for Further Reading

The New American Bible. This is the translation used in the lectionary. You may also want to have the *New Revised Standard Version* or the *New Jerusalem Bible* as alternative and well-regarded translations to help you get the full flavor of a reading.

The New World Dictionary-Concordance to the New American Bible. World Bible Publishers, 1970.

_____. *At Home with the Word.* Chicago, IL: Liturgy Training Publications.

_____. *Workbook for Lectors and Gospel Readers.* Liturgy Training Publications.

Boudreau, Paul. *Between Sundays: Daily Gospel Reflections and Prayers.* Mystic, CT: Twenty-Third Publications, 2001.

Brueggemann, Walter. *The Bible Makes Sense,* rev. ed. Winona, MN: Saint Mary's Press, 1997.

Camille, Alice. *God's Word Is Alive: Entering the Sunday Readings.* Mystic, CT: Twenty-Third Publications, 1998.

McKenzie, John L. *Dictionary of the Bible.* New York, NY: Simon and Schuster, 1995.

New Jerome Bible Handbook, The. Edited by Raymond Brown, et. al. Collegeville, MN: Liturgical Press, 1992.

Nolan, Albert. *Jesus Before Christianity,* rev. ed. Maryknoll, NY: Orbis Books, 1992.

Exploring the Sunday Readings, a monthly serial commentary. Mystic, CT: Twenty-Third Publications.

The Bible Collection. Videocassettes of fundamental stories of the Hebrew Scriptures. Titles available are *Abraham, Jacob, Joseph, Moses, Samson and Delilah,* and *David.* Turner Home Entertainment, 1994.

The Birth of Jesus. Videocassette presented by Stephen Doyle, OFM. Los Angeles: Franciscan Communications, 1987.

Jesus the Prophet. Videocassette presented by Stephen Doyle. Franciscan Communications, 1987.

Paul, Apostle to the Church Today, Vols. I-II. Videocassettes by Stephen Doyle. Franciscan Communications, 1988.